Cubism

by

Annie Sanders

Dreamschooner Press

ISBN 978-0-9840527-9-0

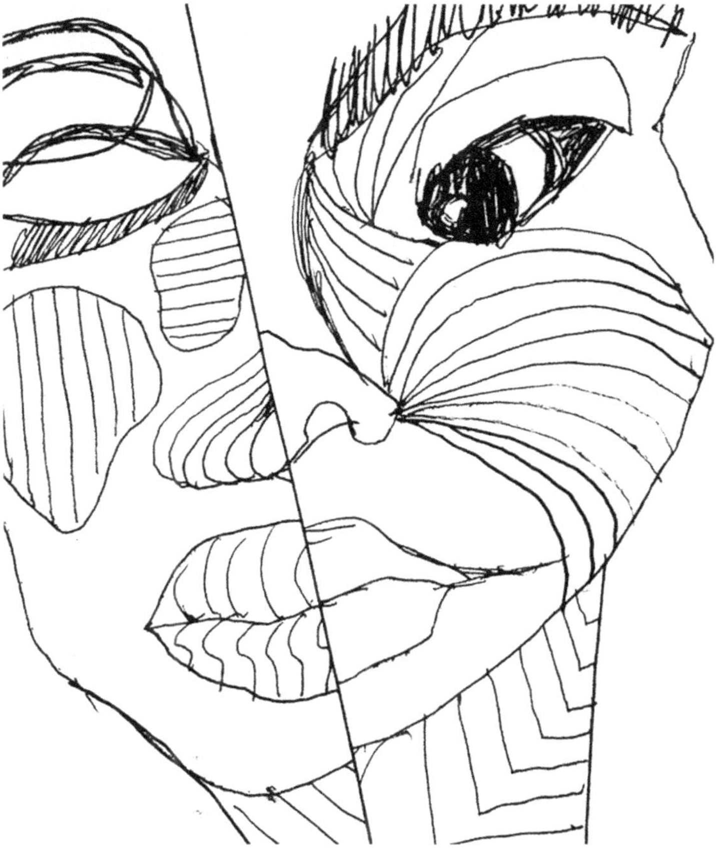

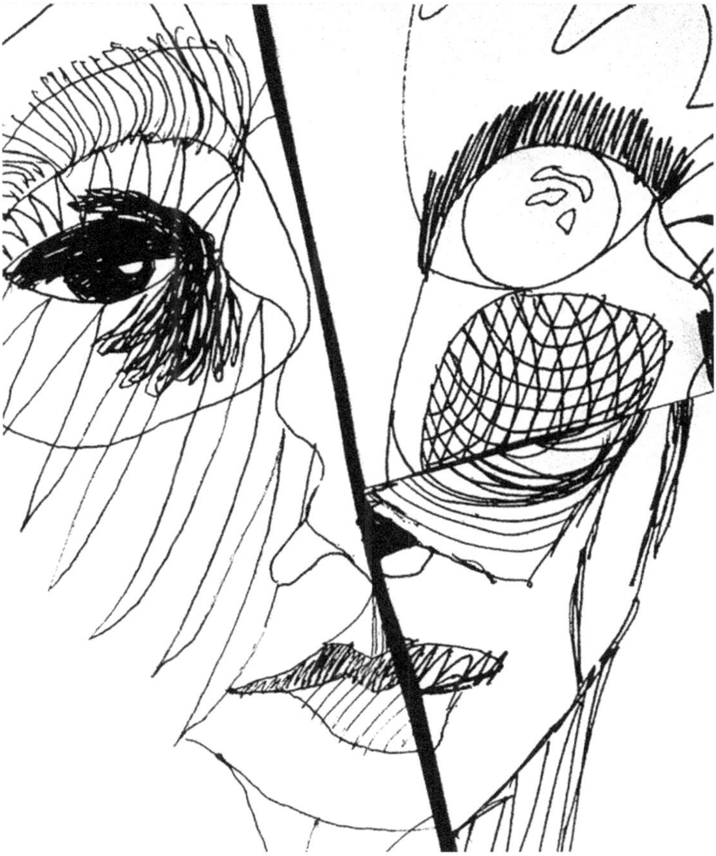

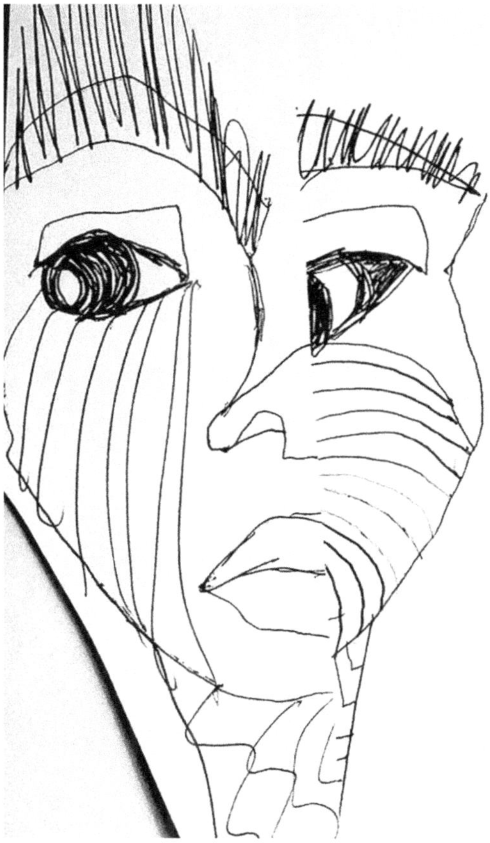

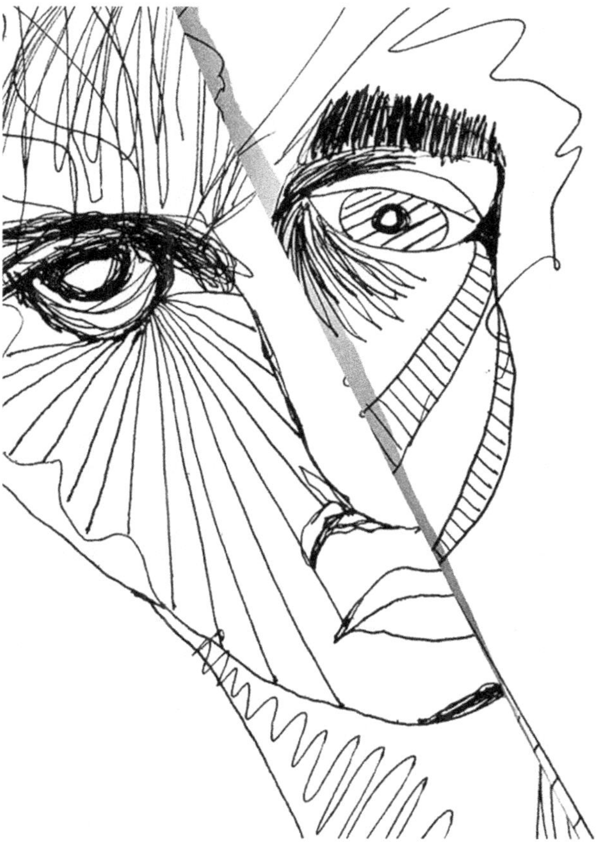

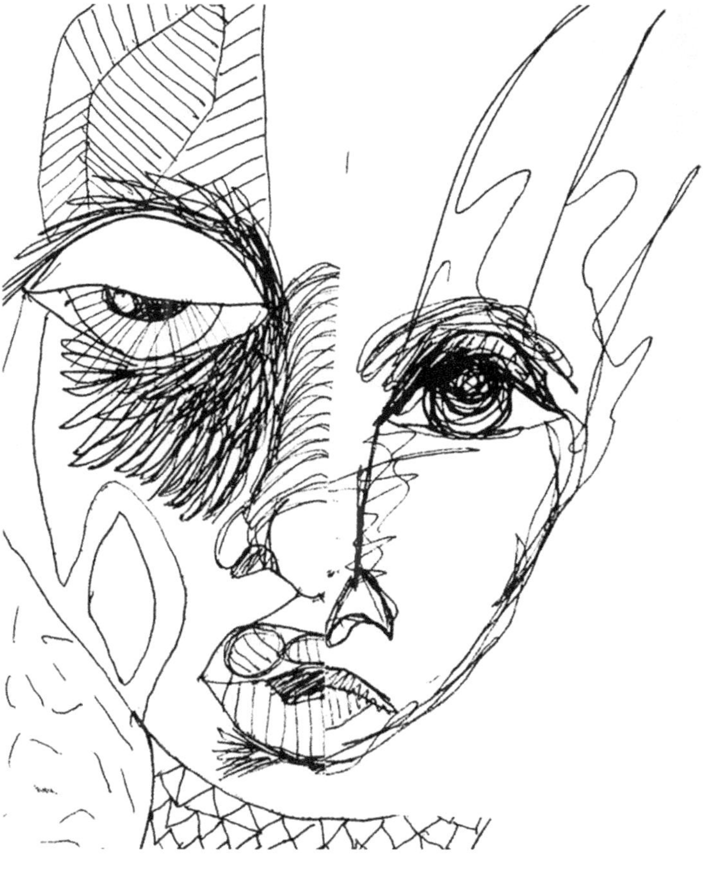

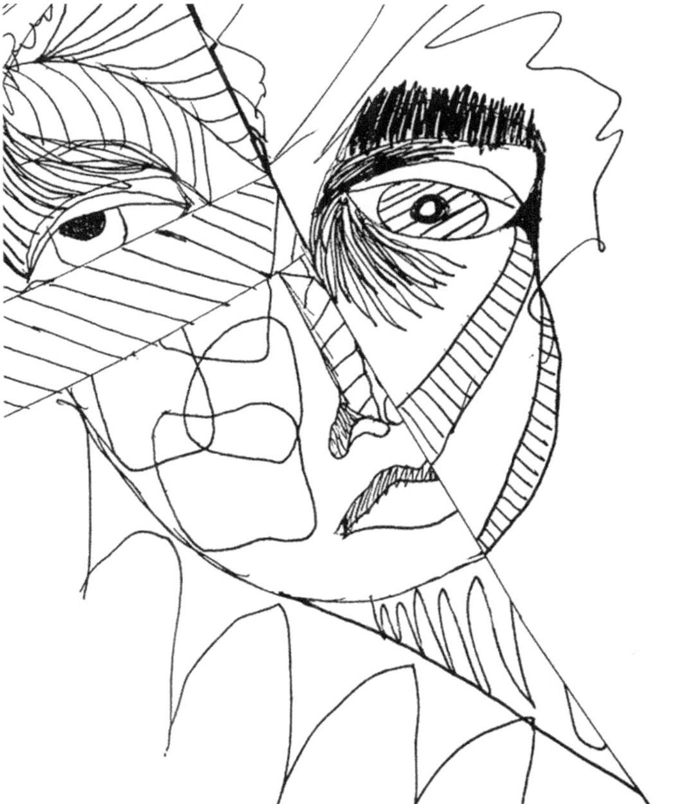

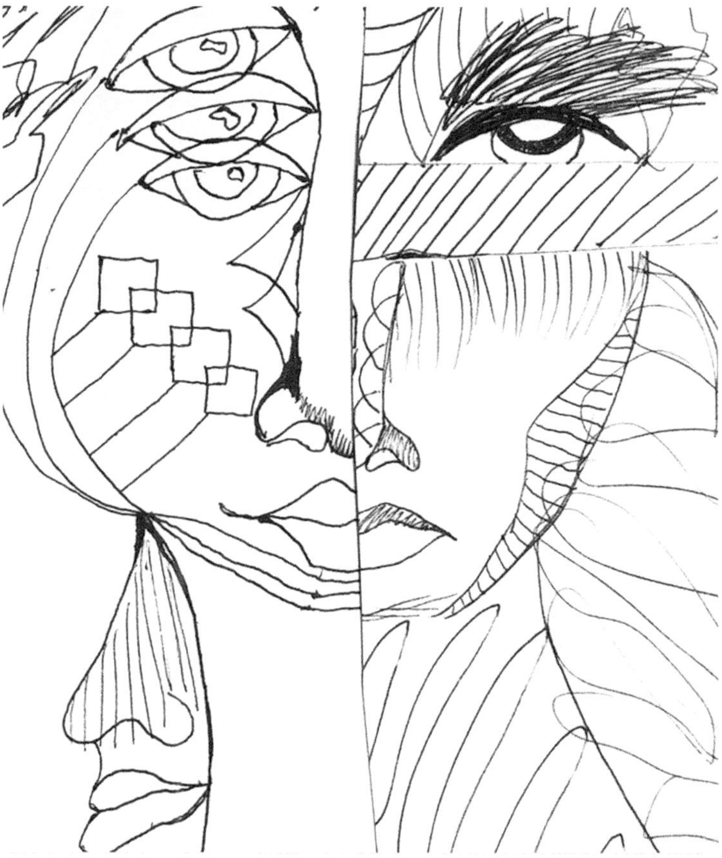

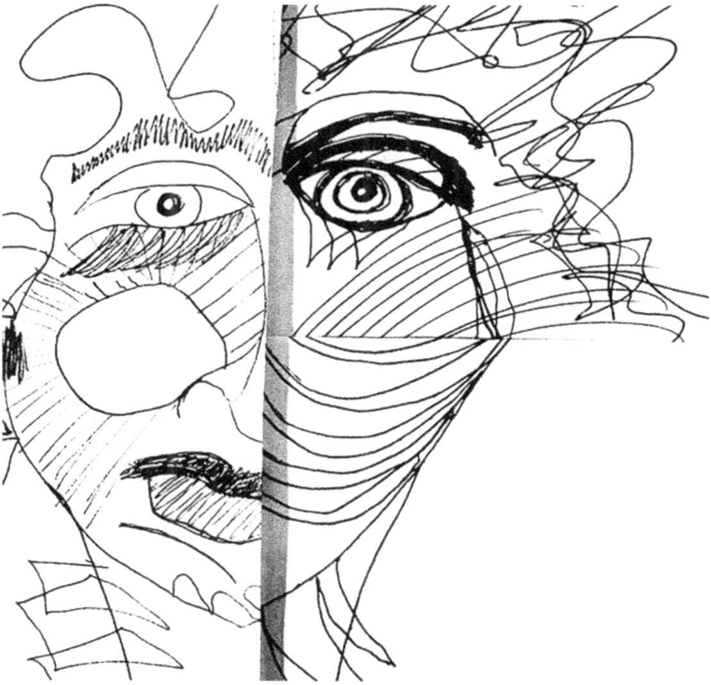

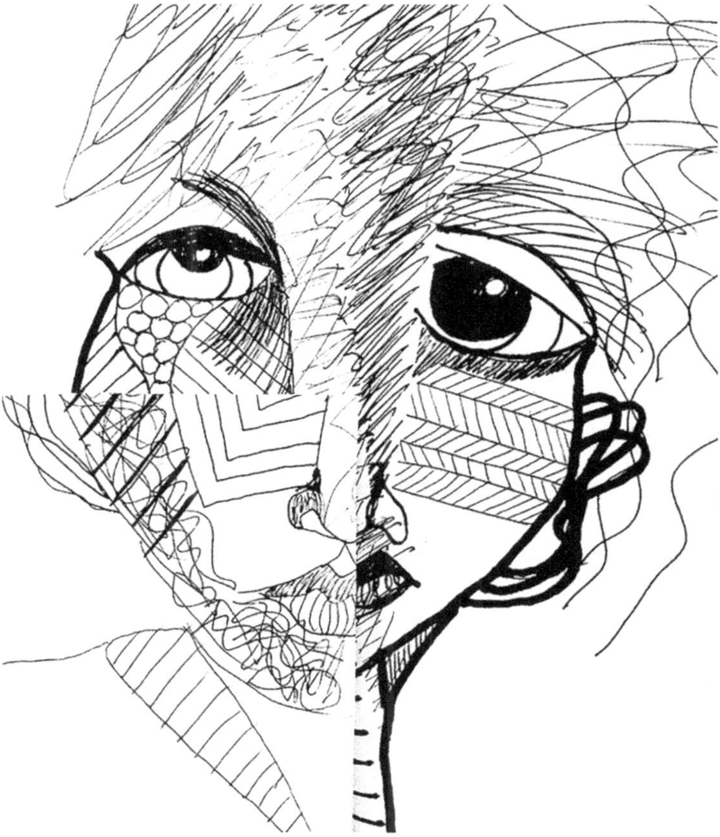

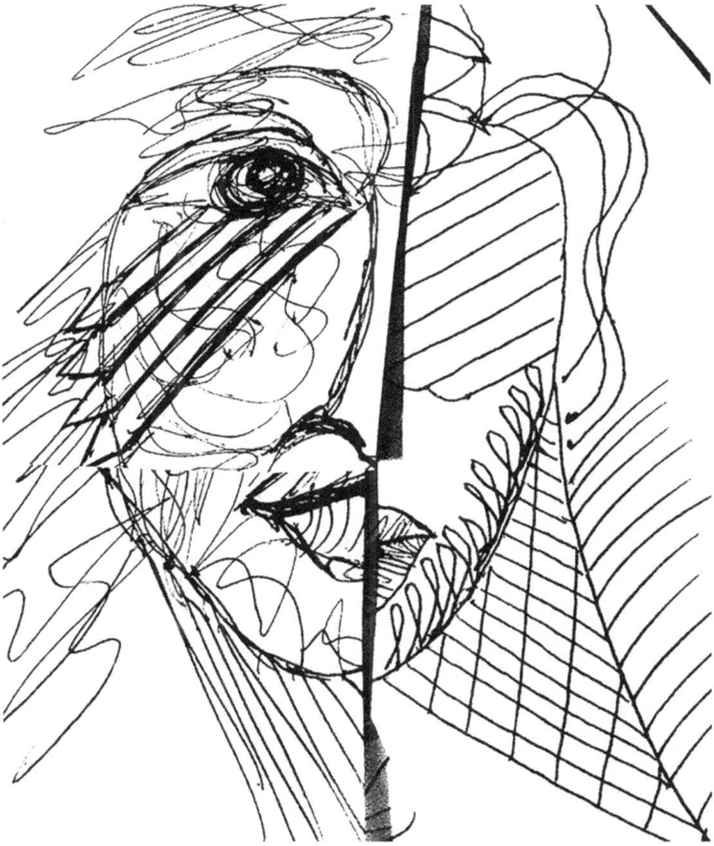

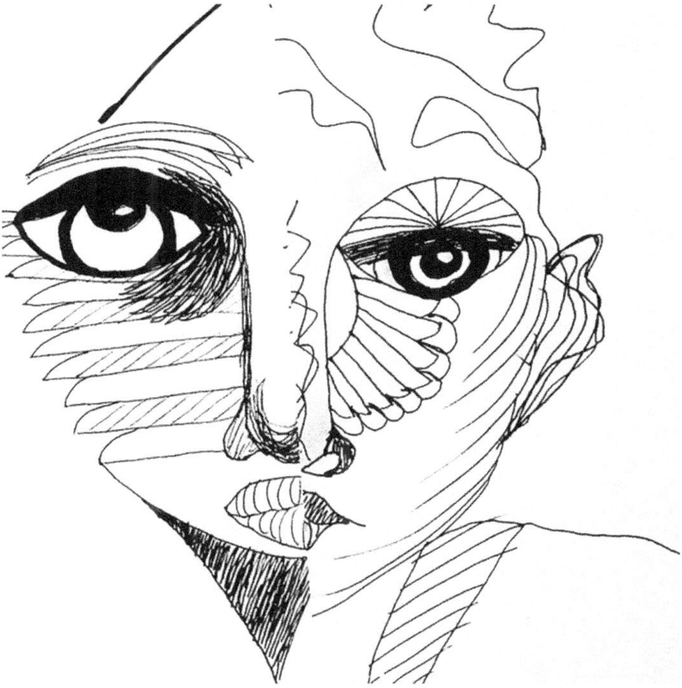

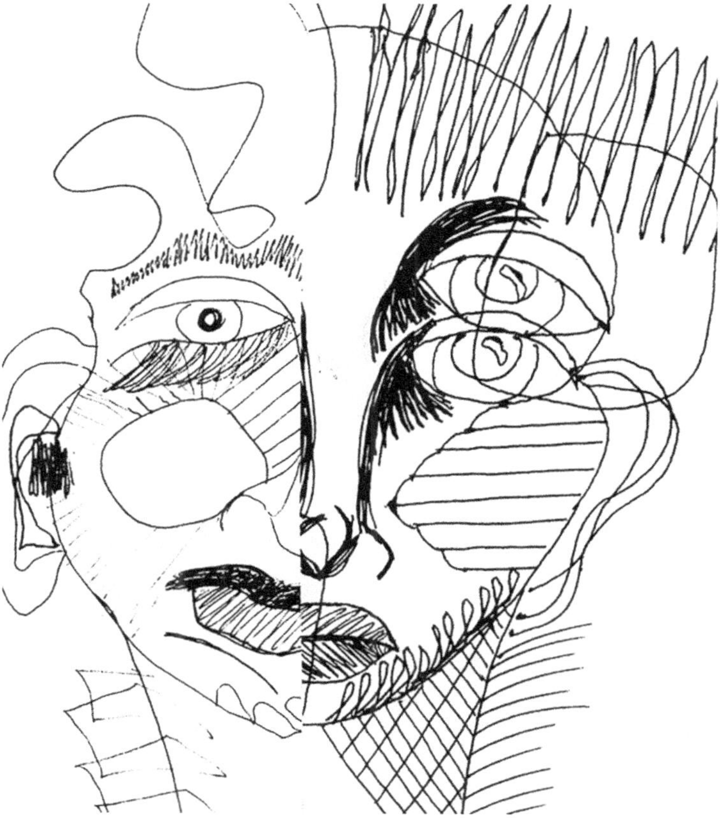

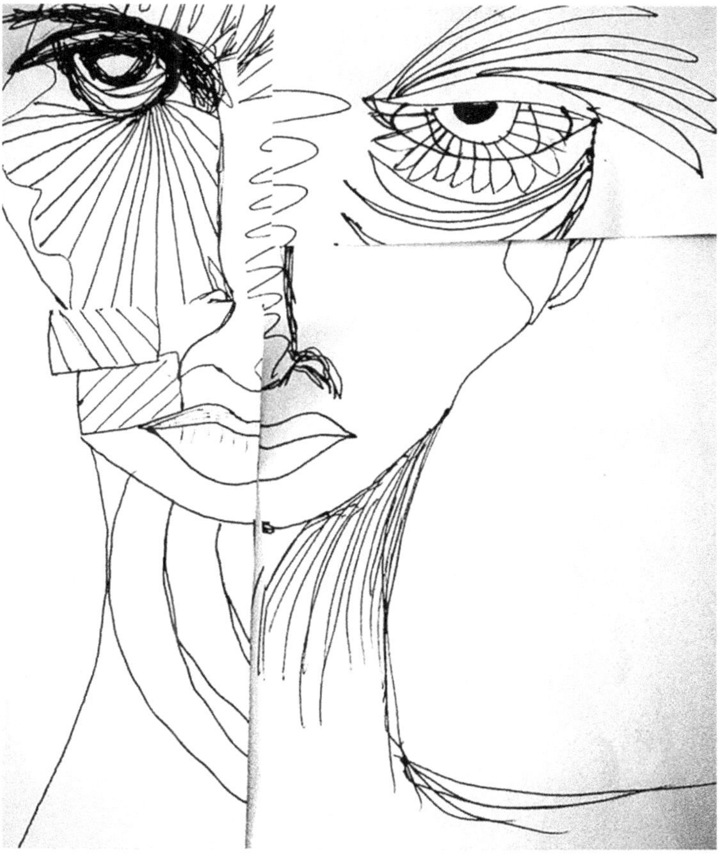

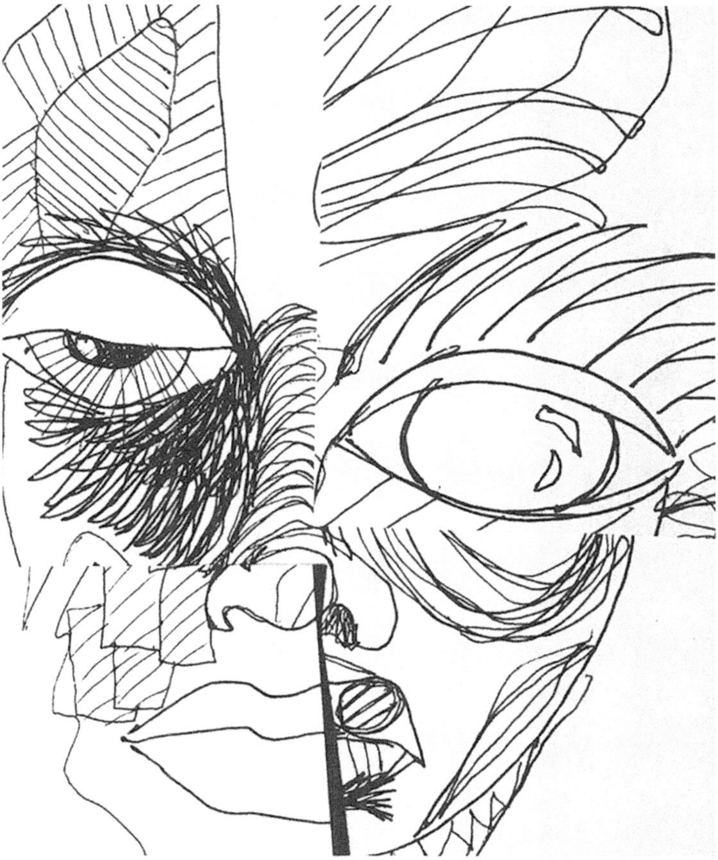

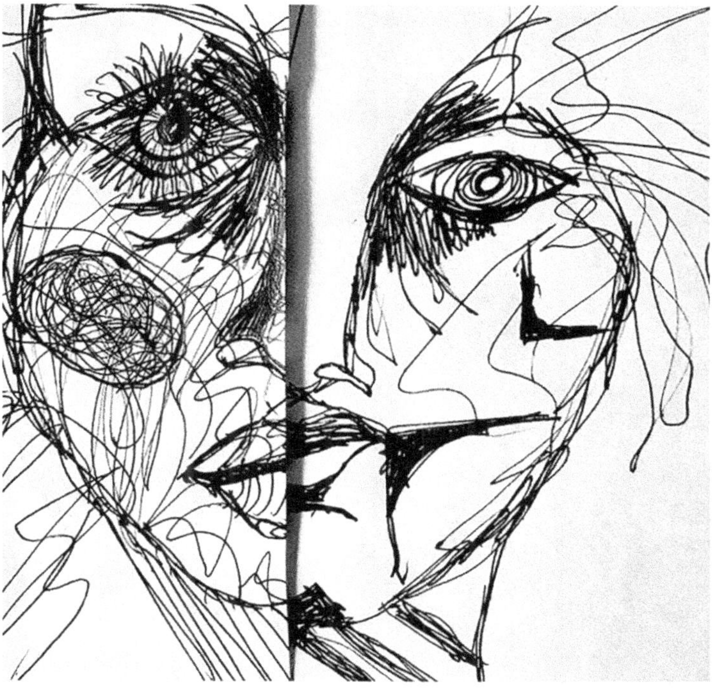

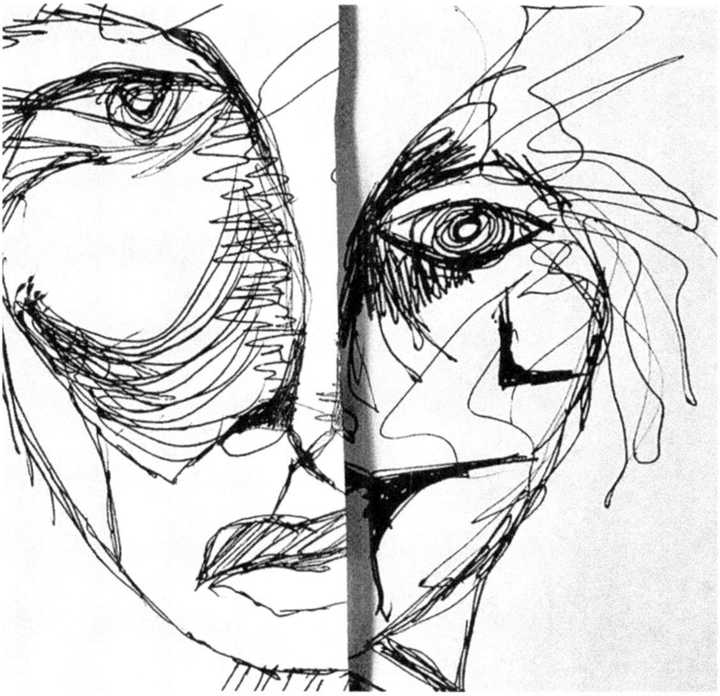

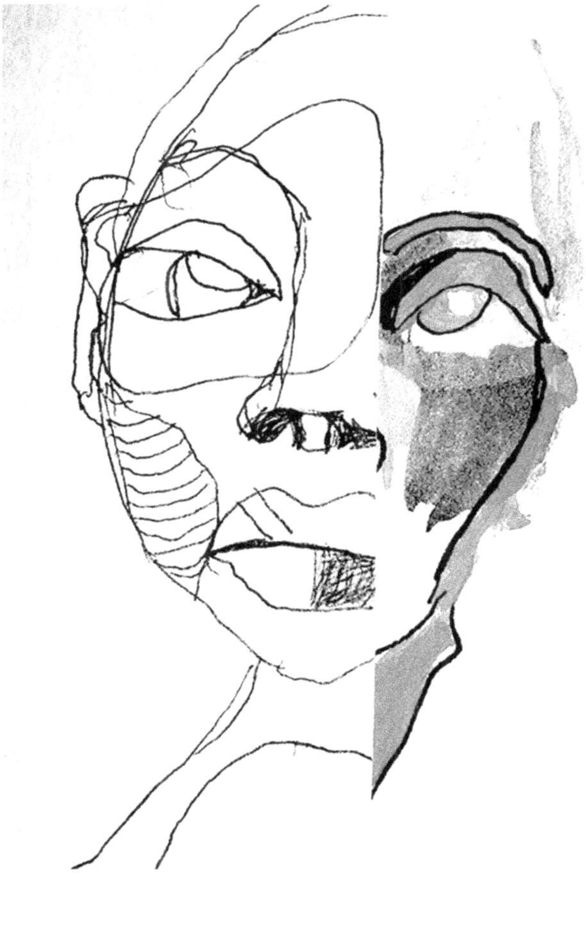

www.ingramcontent.com/pod-product-compliance
Lightning Source LLC
Chambersburg PA
CBHW072305170526
45158CB00003BA/1202
* 9 7 8 0 9 8 4 0 5 2 7 9 0 *